Kevin Mayhew

We hope you enjoy *Sight-Singing Made Easy*.
Further copies are available from your local music shop.

In case of difficulty, please contact the publisher direct:

The Sales Department
KEVIN MAYHEW LTD
Rattlesden
Bury St Edmunds
Suffolk IP30 0SZ

Phone 0449 737978
Fax 0449 737834

Please ask for our complete catalogue of outstanding Instrumental and Vocal Music.

First published in Great Britain in 1994 by Kevin Mayhew Ltd

© Copyright 1994 Kevin Mayhew Ltd

ISBN 0 86209 571 9
Catalogue No: 3611131

The music and texts in this book are protected by copyright and may not be reproduced
in any way for sale or private use without the consent of the copyright owner.

Cover design by Tom Hewitt
Music Editor: Anthea Smith
Music setting by Tricia Oliver

Printed and bound in Great Britain

Foreword

The ability to sing at sight is one of the marks of a good musician. It is the starting point for hearing a piece of music simply by reading the manuscript, and it develops the ability to spot mistakes in one's own playing.

Sight-singing is an essential skill for singers. It is also a useful tool for anyone sitting examinations which include an aural section, particularly as some examination boards have introduced sight-singing as part of the aural tests for some grades, and musicianship examinations may also require it. A study of this book will give the skill and confidence to tackle sight-singing with ease.

Whatever your voice is like, it is still possible to sing musically as long as you sing legato, keep a regular tempo and breathe only between phrases. A knowledge of clefs, note names and simple rhythm is assumed. It will be helpful if some scales and arpeggios have already been played, but this is not essential.

Sets of exercises are presented in both treble and bass clefs. They are not intended as alternatives, but should all be worked through, singing them at a convenient octave – the more you do, the better you get. Singing an arpeggio puts you in touch with the harmonic basis of a key, and also places you within one degree of all other notes of the scale. Once the ability to pitch any note of the scale has been established, accompaniments have been provided for the last two exercises in each group. These take the format of either a simple countermelody or a straightforward piano part.

It is recommended that you do not leave a section until you can accomplish it easily; each one builds on the skills already mastered.

JANET BAILEY

CHAPTER 1

> AIM   To learn to sing and to recognise the notes of the arpeggios in various keys.
>
> METHOD
> - Listen carefully to the chord.
> - Sing the notes to their letter names.
> - Sing smoothly and evenly at a steady speed.
> - Sing the whole exercise in one breath.
> - If the range is wrong for your voice, do not struggle but change the pitch. An octave up or down is the simplest, but you could transpose into any convenient key whilst continuing to read the letter names on the printed page.
> - Repeat each section until you are confident before you go on.

1. Arpeggios in the major keys with key signatures of up to two sharps or flats.

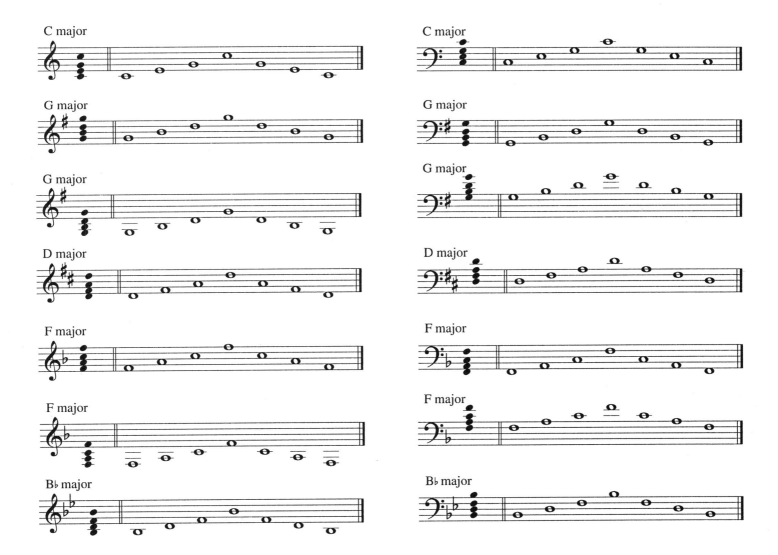

2. Arpeggios in the minor keys with key signatures of up to two sharps or flats.

The third of the key is a semitone lower in a minor arpeggio; for example G major has B♮ but G minor has B♭.

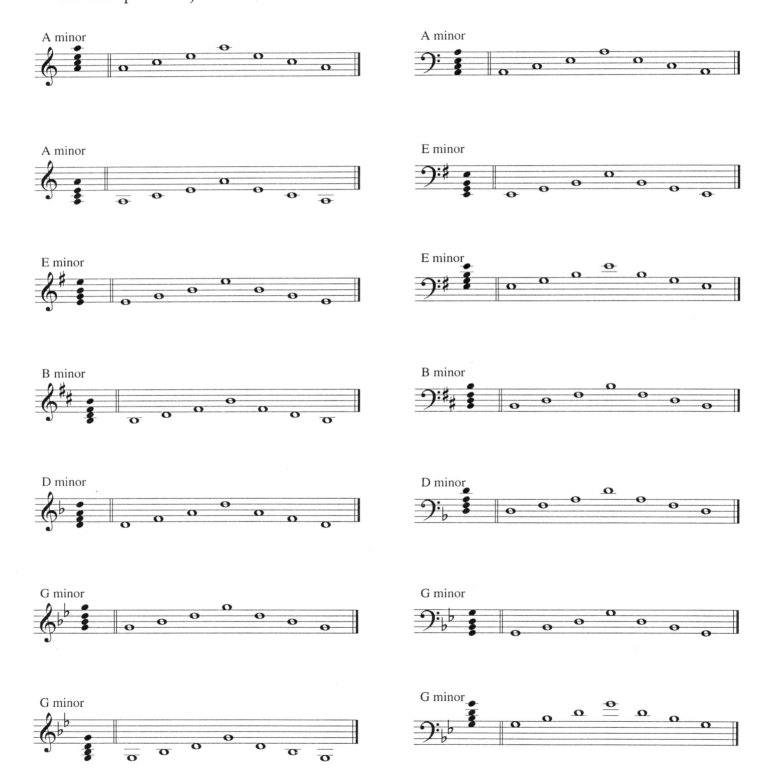

3. Major and minor keys mixed.

Work out whether the key is major or minor *before* you listen to the chord.

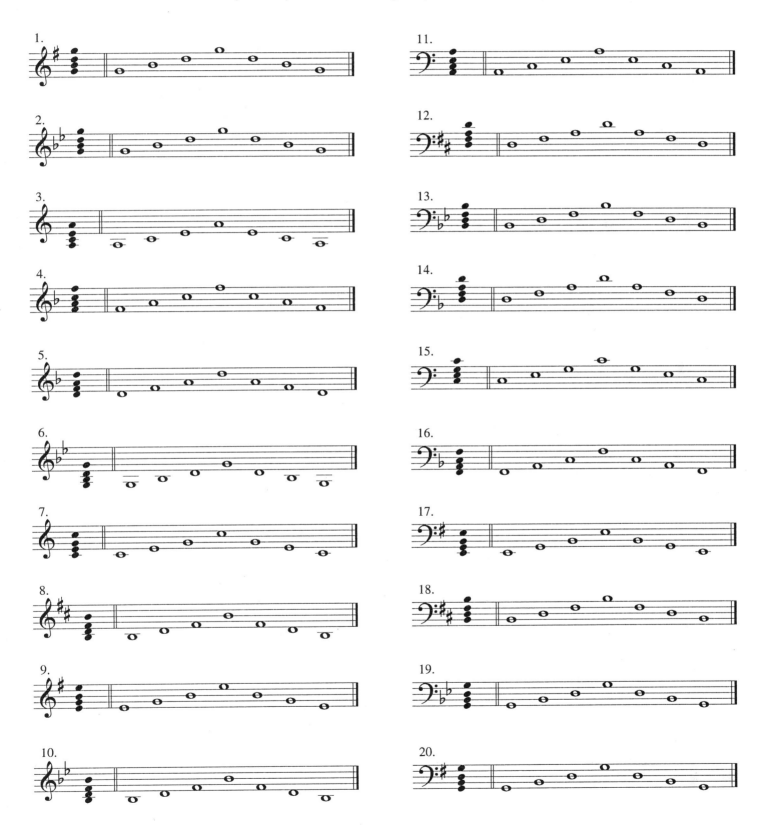

4. Major keys, singing down and up.

Do not cheat by singing up first!

1.

2.
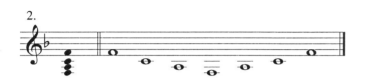

3.

4.
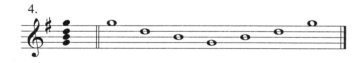

5.

6.

7.
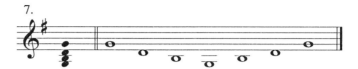

8.

9.

10.
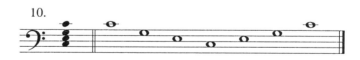

11.

12.

5. Minor keys, singing down and up.

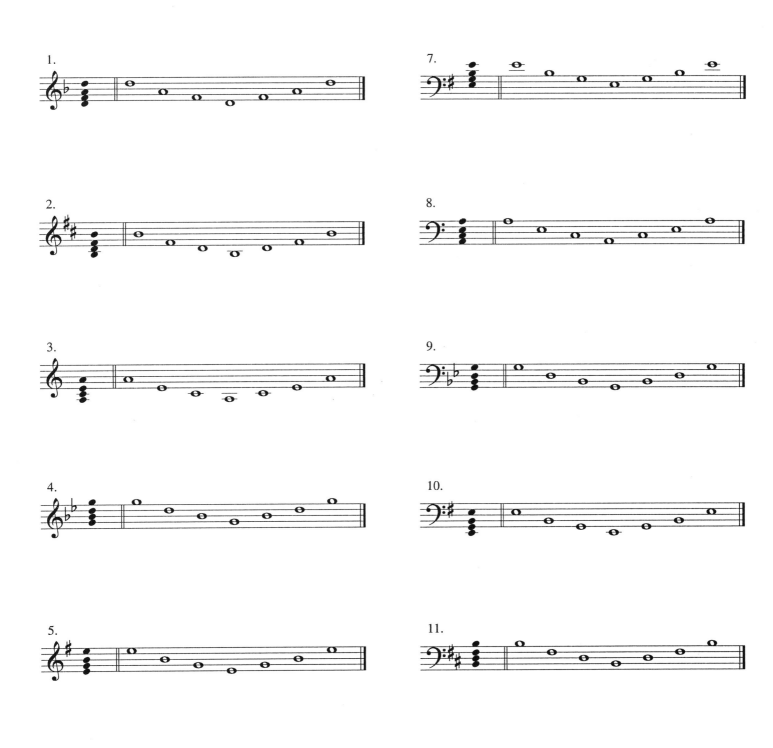

6. Major and minor keys mixed, singing down and up.

Work out the key *before* you hear the chord.

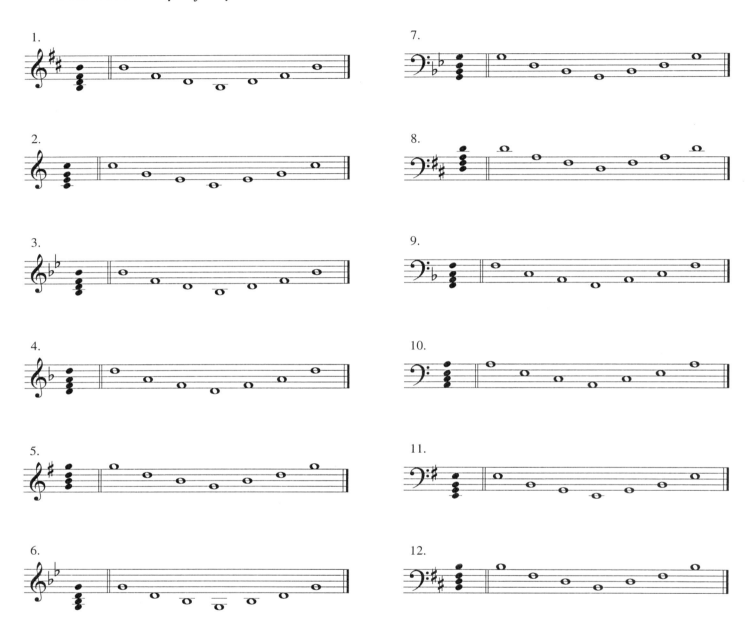

7. Learning to pitch from the keynote alone.

This is a very important skill. Go back to the beginning of the chapter and repeat all the exercises, being given the keynote only. Sing to 'vah' instead of the notenames, repeating each section until you are confident.

8. A mixture of exercises, summing up the chapter.

Listen to the *keynote only* before you sing. Sing to 'vaw'.
N.B. You will find this section difficult if you skipped Section 7!

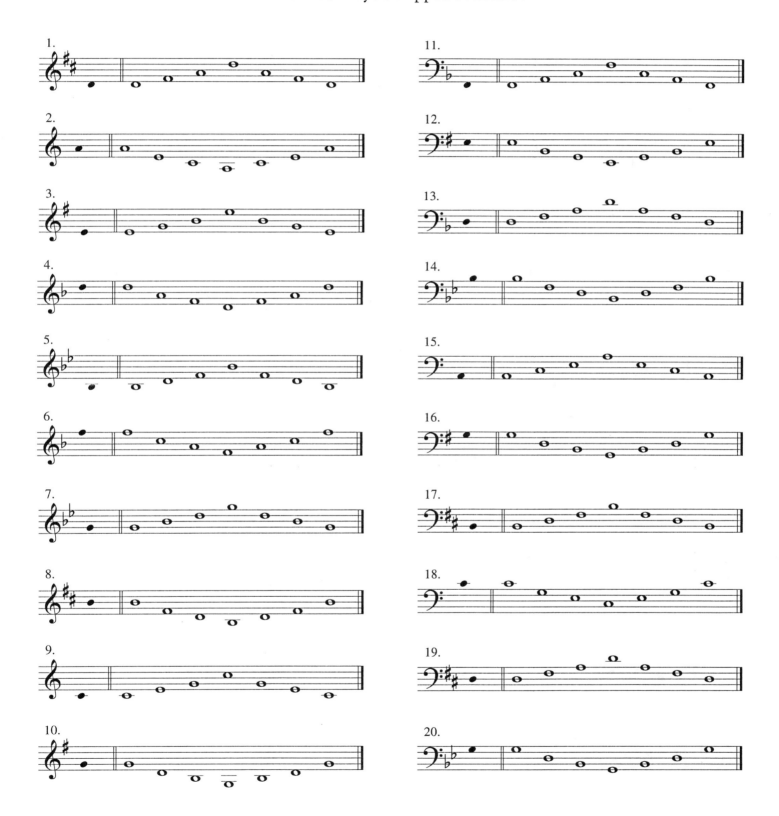

CHAPTER 2

> AIM To sing the arpeggio notes in any order, using simple rhythms.
>
> METHOD
> - From now on, sound the keynote only before singing.
> - Continue to sing the exercises to the note names if there is the slightest uncertainty. Otherwise, choose from 'vaw', 'vah' or 'lah', using whichever suits you best.
> - Remember your legato.
> - You should only need one breath for each exercise.

1. Arpeggios in both major and minor keys with simple rhythm added.

   Count one bar in to set the speed.

2. Changes of direction and missed notes in major keys, using common time.

3. Changes of direction and missed notes in minor keys, using common time.

14

4. Major and minor keys mixed, using 3/4 time.

CHAPTER 3

> AIM To add the second and fourth degrees of the scale to the arpeggio.
>
> METHOD
> - Use the arpeggio notes as stepping stones to the new notes.
> - Be clear which are the arpeggio notes in each exercise before you sing.
> - The second and fourth notes are the same whether the key is major or minor.
> - Note that the exercises are grouped with the major keys first.

1. Arpeggios with either the second or fourth added.

Major keys

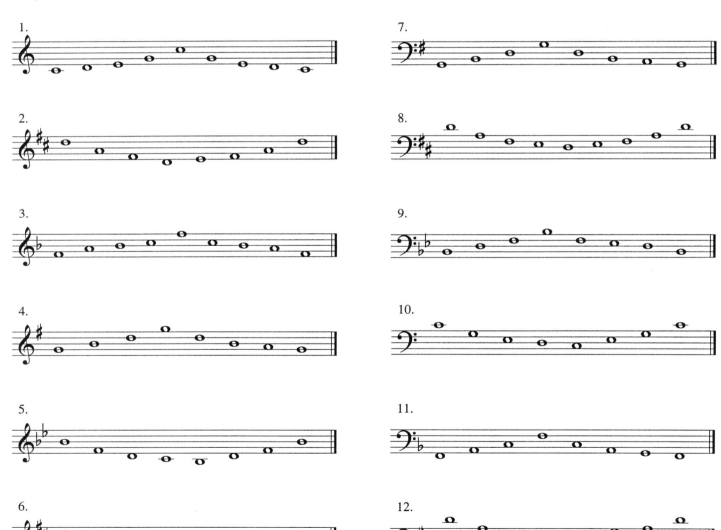

Minor keys

13.

19.

14.

20.

15.

21.

16.

22.

17.
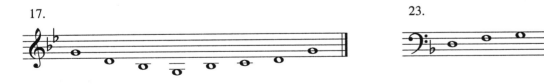

23.

18.

24.

2. Arpeggios with both the second and fourth added.

Major keys

1.

4.

2.

5.

3.

6.

Minor keys

7.

10.

8.

11.

9.

12.

3. Changes of direction.

Major keys

Minor keys

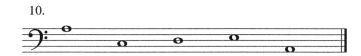

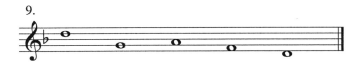

4. Simple rhythm added.

Use one breath for each phrase.

CHAPTER 4

> AIM To add the sixth degree of the scale to the arpeggio.
>
> METHOD
> - Remember the sixth is just one step up from the fifth, although there is a difference between major and minor keys. For example, the sixth degree of G major is E♮ while in G minor it is E♭. A study of the harmonic minor scale will make this clear.
> - Use only one breath per phrase.
> - Note that from Section 3 onwards, arpeggio notes may be used in new octaves. For example, exercise 12 in Section 3 has a B above the stave in G major, and exercise 9 in Section 4 uses D, fourth line up, in B♭ major.
> - Always check for *all* arpeggio notes before you begin.

1. Arpeggios with the sixth added.

Major keys

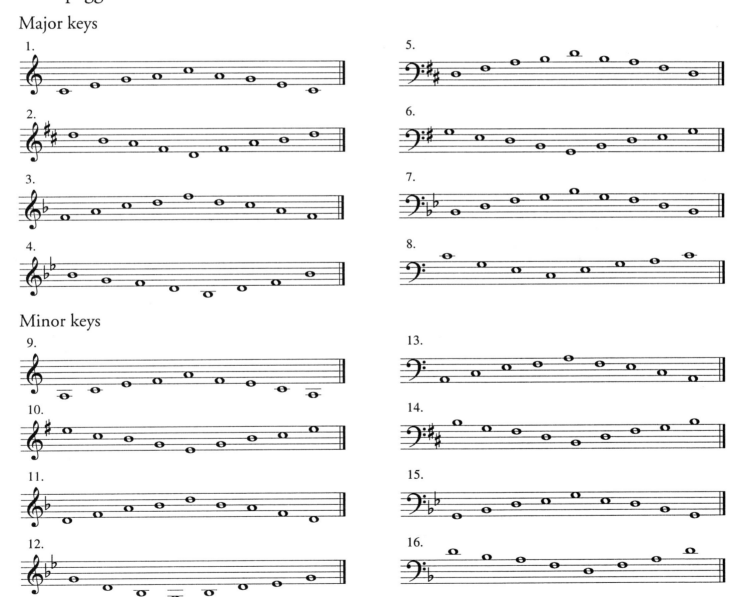

Minor keys

2. Arpeggios with the sixth added,
   plus the second and/or the fourth.

Major keys

1.

9.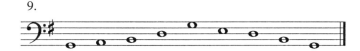

2.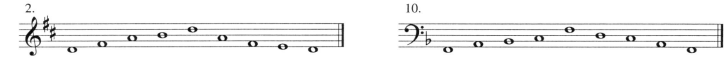

10.

3.

11.

4.

12.

5.

13.

6.

14.

7.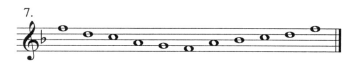

15.

8.

16.

Minor keys

17.

25.

18.

26.
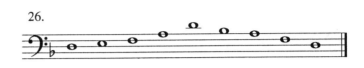

19.

27.

20.

28.

21.

29.

22.

30.

23.

31.
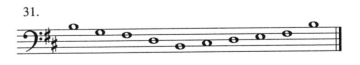

24.

32.

3. Changes of direction.

Major keys

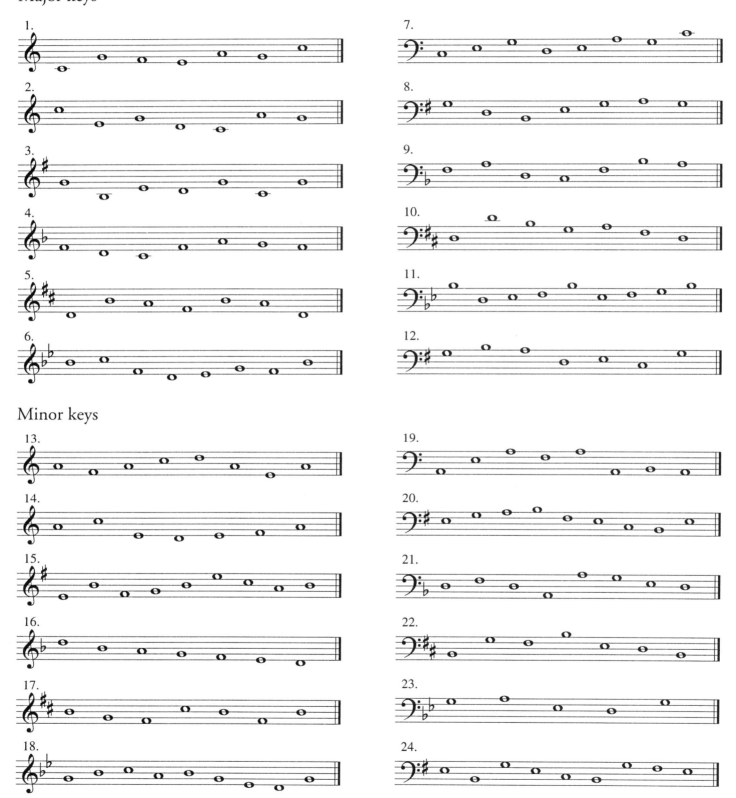

Minor keys

4. Simple rhythm added.

Set a steady pulse first.

25

CHAPTER 5

> AIM — To add the seventh degree of the scale.
>
> METHOD
> - Connect the seventh note of the scale to the keynote.
> - The harmonic version of the minor scale is the only one used in this book, so the seventh note of the scale is the same in both major and minor keys.
> - Remember your legato.

1. Arpeggios with the seventh added.

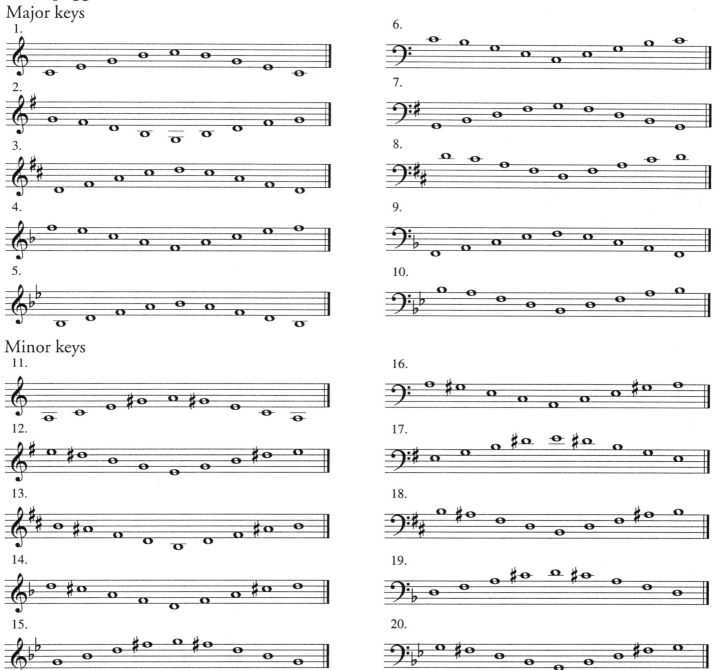

2. Using all notes of the scale.

Major keys

1.

2.

3.

4.

5.

6.

Minor keys

7.

8.

9.
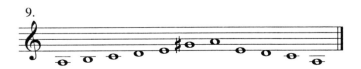

10.

11.

12.
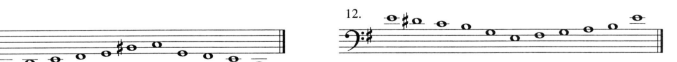

3. Changes of direction.

Major keys

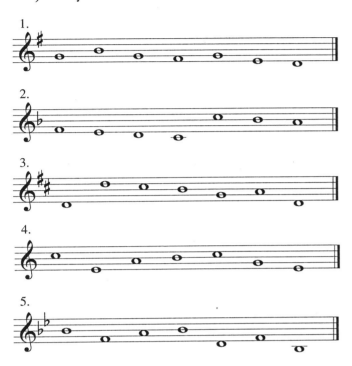
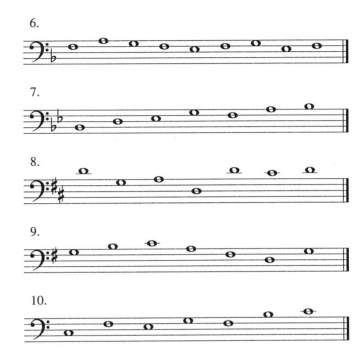

Minor keys

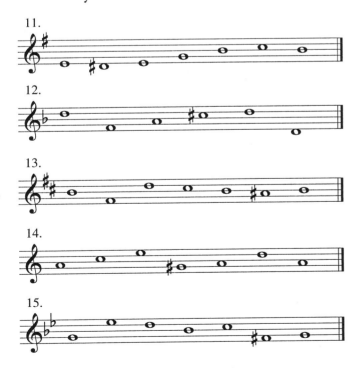
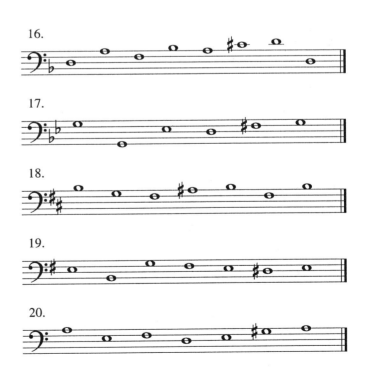

4. Simple rhythm added.

From here on the last two exercises in each group have optional accompaniments. The first one is always a single line which can be sung or played by the teacher in any convenient octave. The second is for piano or keyboard.
Breathe between the phrases.

CHAPTER 6

> AIM To introduce quaver patterns.
>
> METHOD
> - Count a bar in, including the quavers in your counting. Two possible methods are counting either '1 and 2 and', or the French time names 'ta te ta te'.
> - Always identify the notes of the arpeggio before you start an exercise.
> - Some of the melodies given in this and subsequent chapters are well-known tunes. Can you identify the pieces marked with an asterisk? Answers are given on page 88.

1. Melodies with pairs of quavers.

33

2. Melodies with dotted crotchets and quavers.

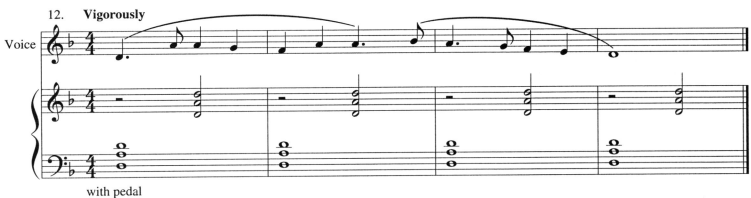

3. Melodies with a mixture of rhythms.

A mixture of major and minor keys too!

CHAPTER 7

> AIM To add semiquavers to the rhythms already introduced.
>
> METHOD
> - A slower speed is needed to cope with the semiquavers.
> - Take extra care counting long notes – it is all too easy to hurry them.
> - Look where to breathe before you begin each exercise.

1. Melodies with groups of four semiquavers.

2. Melodies with groups of quavers and semiquavers.

Be careful to distinguish between ♪♫ and ♫♪

45

3. Melodies with groups of dotted quavers and semiquavers.

CHAPTER 8

AIM — To learn four new keys, and to use the upbeat (anacrusis).

METHOD
- Sing to the note names as in Chapter 1. Be sure of these before you go on to Section 2.
- In Section 3 remember to check which beat of the bar the melody starts on.

1. Arpeggios in the major and minor keys with key signatures of three sharps or flats.

A major

A major

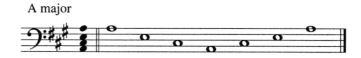

A major

F# minor

F# minor

F# minor

Eb major

Eb major

Eb major

C minor

C minor

2. Melodies in the new keys.

Notice whether there are two or three phrases and breathe accordingly.

3. Melodies in all keys with key signatures of up to three sharps or flats.

They all start with an upbeat.

CHAPTER 9

> AIM To introduce compound time signatures.
>
> METHOD
> - Compound time is based on groups of three.
> - Emphasize the first note of each group to give the main beats of the bar.
> - Keep a steady pulse.

1. Melodies in $\frac{6}{8}$ and $\frac{9}{8}$ time.

    The main beat is a dotted crotchet divided into three quavers.

2. Melodies in 6/8 and 9/8 time, using dotted quavers and semiquavers.

3. Melodies in 6/4 and 9/4 time.

The main beat is a dotted minim divided into three crotchets.

CHAPTER 10

AIM To learn four more new keys.
To introduce some less common time signatures.
To use ties.

METHOD
- Study the new keys as for Chapter 1.
- Take time over the first group of exercises so that you can instantly recognise the arpeggio notes in a melody, whatever the key.
- Make sure that you understand the value of the beat in the new time signatures.
- If ties cause difficulty, sing through the exercise once omitting them.
- Think about your breathing before you begin, and keep a steady pulse.

1. Arpeggios in the major and minor keys with key signatures of four sharps or flats.

E major

E major

C♯ minor

C♯ minor

A♭ major

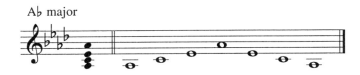

A♭ major

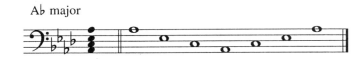

F minor

F minor

2. Melodies in the new keys, using
   all the time signatures studied so far.

3. Melodies in all keys with key signatures of up to four sharps or flats, using ties.

4. Melodies in 2/2, 3/2 and 3/8 time.

3/2 and 2/2 have *minim* beats.
3/8 has *quaver* beats.

CHAPTER 11

AIM To introduce rests and more difficult anacruses.

METHOD
- Music without rests is like language without punctuation – difficult to understand. Please do not ignore them.
- To deal with the upbeats, work out exactly which beat or part-beat you are starting on, and count in carefully.

1. Melodies with rests.

2. Melodies with more difficult anacruses.

CHAPTER 12: FOLKSONGS

A chance to try some longer melodies with words.

EVENING PRAYER

Robin Adair

THE LOYAL LOVER

BARBARA ALLEN

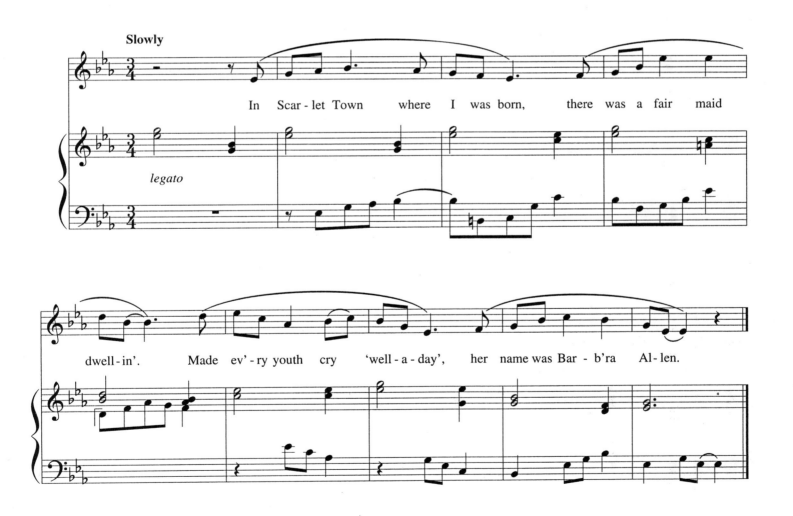

THE VALE OF CLWYD

Robin-a-Thrush

ANSWERS

Chapter 6	Section 1: 5	Sing a song of sixpence
	Section 3: 10	Alouette
Chapter 7	Section 2: 14	This old man
	Section 3: 4	Charlie is my darling
	Section 3: 20	Green grow the rushes
Chapter 8	Section 2: 5	Loudly proclaim
	Section 3: 3	The Ash Grove
	Section 3: 7	Do you ken John Peel
	Section 3: 15	My love's an arbutus
	Section 3: 16	London's burning
Chapter 9	Section 1: 5	Do you plant you cauliflowers
	Section 1: 15	Pop goes the weasel
Chapter 10	Section 2: 4	Boys and girls come out to play
	Section 2: 16	Hot cross buns
Chapter 11	Section 1: 10	A frog he would a-wooing go
	Section 1: 13	On Ilkley Moor baht'at
	Section 2: 4	Londonderry Air
	Section 2: 9	The Keel Row
	Section 2: 21	The Sailor's Hornpipe